Self-Esteem

How To Become Confident And Motivate Yourself In Any Situation & A Manual To Assist You In Regaining Your Confidence By Overcoming Low Self-Esteem And Resolving Inner Conflicts

(Put An End To Victimization And Raise Your Self-Esteem)

KarlheinzWulf

TABLE OF CONTENT

Work On Human Interaction 1

Strive For Excellence By Taking Chances 14

Weaving New Dreams: Plans That Do Not Include Anyone Else. 18

Reduction Of Anxiety And Stress 24

Honouring The Journey 36

Creating A Positive Attitude 51

The Thing We Refer To As Emotions 74

How To Encourage Conversations With Those Around You 88

The Benefits Of Having Positive Dialogues With Yourself 121

Work On Human Interaction

Your words make the difference if your body language positions you for success. It's one of the hardest things to accomplish since you must speak those thoughts out loud inside your head. If you weren't paralyzed with terror earlier, now is most likely the moment to do so.

Either you stop talking or lose track of what you were saying. Perhaps you're attempting to organize your ideas into a coherent sentence, but instead, you wind up using many "us" or falling back on your colloquialisms. Your gaze darts about the room, and what you see is an enormous catastrophe. Whatever you do, it always sounds like you don't know what you're discussing. Now, let's discuss those.

Establishing eye contact is the first step. It is impossible to glance away from the individuals you are speaking with and at anything else in the room. While maintaining steady eye contact doesn't require you to lock eyes and stare, it does convey your confidence and desire for people to listen to what you have to say.

The second step is to pay attention to who you are speaking with. When someone outside your social group uses your vocabulary, you could find it offensive, but you must consider how it makes them feel. Avoid using slang when interacting with others, especially those you don't know, as you want them to appreciate and understand you.

Making eye contact, speaking clearly and succinctly, avoiding slang, and using appropriate body language are excellent places to start, but they won't assist you when all you can say is "um." So, how can you support that to give off an air of confidence?

I can share one piece of advice based on personal experience. I had very low confidence and was looking for new friends. I didn't know what to do because I didn't feel confident, but I knew that others would be wary of me if I continued to be shy. I would practise in front of my mirror as a result. I would hold myself in how I desired to be perceived. I would then simulate speaking with my peers. My screenplay eventually became second nature to me, and I was pleasantly delighted when it performed.

That practice wasn't always what I wanted others to see. It was an actual feeling I had.

Acquire Some Expert Understanding

You must be somewhat knowledgeable for the words you are uttering to have any real impact. Speaking will become easier for you as you gain knowledge and become an authority. The best method for getting rid of "um" from your vocabulary is this.

Let's imagine you have to give a presentation on a book. What occurs when the time comes for that presentation if you haven't read the book and gained a comprehension of its main themes? Isn't it destined to fail? How about if you simply skim it? You will fumble a lot when you speak, but you might be able to provide some information. The knowledge you gain beforehand is the only thing that will give you confidence during that presentation.

Your confidence will increase with any information you gain on a subject, but what about the times before that?

You should have no trouble admitting when you don't know anything about a subject. When the topic of conversation shifts to something you are not as knowledgeable about, you should be able to admit it to the other person and say you are open to learning more.

Regaining Your Self-Belief

Like low self-esteem, it can be difficult to regain self-confidence once it has been damaged. These are simply unpleasant days, but when you feel unconfident, it affects how you act and behave at home and school. Making your voice heard is hard and can contribute to the loneliness we previously talked about.

By being here and reading this book, you are already going beyond the most difficult part—recognizing that there is a problem in the first place. Upon realizing that we have difficulties with some things, our initial reaction is to solve those issues. You can now put part of what you've learned thus far into practice. The most important one is figuring out what your strengths and limitations are. After you know that, you can focus on your "weak" areas.

You can begin examining the external elements that have impacted your self-confidence after identifying the internal problems. The actions and mindsets of others have the power to destroy your self-esteem. Adults who are harsh with you, including bullies, can impact you. Now is the moment to speak out if any of these variables impact you. Remember that the longer you remain silent, the more difficult it will be for you to heal.

Everyone will tell you that you should always talk to the aggressor first in situations like this. That should be your primary course of action. However, you need to involve someone in a higher authority, such as a coach, parent, or teacher, if you feel that speaking with them will put you at risk. Find another individual who can support you, even if the aggressor is an adult.

Now, refocus the attention back on yourself. You are usually miserable when criticising your worth, confidence, or self-esteem. You believe that you don't deserve happiness, which is a risky way of thinking since it implies that you should be treated poorly and that everyone else should. But you are deserving of pleasure and all those wonderful things. The greatest time to change this feeling is right now, but there is still time! You're capable of it. All you have to do is believe.

We can now concentrate on three strategies to help you regain your confidence after you've evaluated the circumstance and acknowledged that you deserve to be happy. This is genuinely being more confident, not just seeming more confident. While appearance can be fixed temporarily, rebuilding ensures a long-term solution.

GOAL-SETTING MOVEMENTS

Here are some exercises to help you develop intriguing and well-aligned goals. If you read this as an ebook, take a notebook and jot down your answers there. Alternatively, you can write your responses directly on the pages.

Exercise #1: Consider Your Principles

Spend some time thinking about your basic principles. Which values and tenets are most significant to you? List your core principles, such as integrity, originality, or adventure.

Exercise #2: Aligning Goals with Values

List your present objectives and contrast them with your guiding principles. Assess your objectives: Do they reflect your ideals, or must they be realigned to resolve conflicts? If you discover any differences, take some time to reevaluate and reframe those objectives to make sure they are consistent with your values.

Exercise #3: Envision the Future You Want

C Close your eyes and visualise the future you want. In the following five or ten years, see yourself leading a purposeful and happy life. What observations do you have? Which objectives have you fulfilled? Spend some time writing a thorough description of your perfect future, including all the significant things to you, such as your work, relationships, personal development, and way of life. This vivisualizationight inspire you to develop goals that will motivate you to work towards that future.

Exercise #4: Determine Your Interests and Passions

Consider the pursuits and activities that make you happy and stoke your passion. What draws you in naturally? Jot down a list of your hobbies and passions, such as painting, gardening, writing, or performing music. Think about how you can use your passions to further your objectives. Your motivation and enjoyment of the journey will be enhanced when your goals align with your hobbies.

Exercise #5: Make SMART objectives

Use the SMART goal framework to ensure your goals are specific and attainable. You may set objectives that are realistic, focused, and in line with your true desires by using this process. Make a list of objectives that incorporate all of the related elements.

Time-bound, relevant, measurable, achievable, and specific

Exercise #6: Look for Outside Assistance

Contact a coach, mentor, or trusted friend and let them know your objectives. Ask them for their opinions and ideas on whether your objectives are worthwhile and consistent with your beliefs. An outside viewpoint might occasionally offer insightful criticism and assist you in further refining your objectives. Accept the advice and assistance of others as you work through setting meaningful, congruent goals. Determine and jot down the names of these individuals you will correspond with.

Remember that creating goals is a continuous process rather than a one-time event. Plan frequent self-check-ins to review your objectives and see how well they connect with your values and aspirations. As necessary, make changes to ensure that your objectives keep you inspired and motivated. You may stay connected to your objectives and make any necessary course corrections by engaging in this frequent practice of contemplation and modification.

You are starting to set objectives that are not only intriguing but also strongly in line with your values and aspirations with the help of the activities above.

When you strive towards accomplishing your goals, you might have a feeling of purpose and fulfilment when your objectives align with your true values.

Strive For Excellence By Taking Chances

Because happiness entails danger, it's quite simple to put off doing what we want to do in life. Yes, you would prefer to live a terrible existence and pursue a vocation you detest than follow your true happiness. Why do you inquire? Because maintaining the status quo is so cosy. There's a remedy to this, however. We call that risk-taking.

First, if you've pondered taking a risk and opted against it,n you're not alone. Before reaching achievement, most people limit themselves and only think about what can go wrong. Ironically, by exaggerating our imaginations, individuals typically overestimate the likelihood that something would go wrong while dismissing the possible advantages.

Therefore, most people continue their regular daily activities rather than act. But consider this: by staying idle, what are you giving up? You have to take action before things in your life drastically alter. Playing it safe keeps you where you've always been, even while the problems in your life get worse.

What is the process of learning to take risks?

Make a plan for your course of action.

Trust that you will be successful.

Put your plan into action.

Analyse how well you performed.

Rethink and move on to the next objective.

It is easy, isn't it? You'll start to see the advantages of pursuing your objectives and desires rather than waiting for them to find you if you start evaluating the benefits equally with the drawbacks.

Chapter 21: Allocating Your Profits

It's time to start investing after your savings have increased. Naturally, set aside a portion for an emergency fund. It's time to break free from your entrenched perspective if you think investing is hard! It's incredibly easy to do with mutual funds, which more than 40% of American households invest in. You simply choose a set of firms you'd want to invest in, and BOOM, you have a diversified portfolio of stocks. This is how investing may be done from the convenience of your own home.

I. Put aside $500–$1,000.

II. Research brokerage accounts online. Research the benefits and drawbacks of each before deciding which account to open.

III. Fill out the online application for a brokerage account and wait for approval.

IV. Add money to your account and decide how it will be invested.

Investing may be made simple, as you can see. A reliable advisor should always be consulted beforehand as they may have further suggestions. Your perspective on money should quickly shift once you've mastered the art of saving and investing!

Weaving New Dreams: Plans That Do Not Include Anyone Else.

The chance to create new ambitions and goals independent of another person's affection or presence arises when someone overcomes unrequited love. This thirteenth chapter will discuss the significance of developing personal plans and objectives that support emotional fulfilment and personal development. By setting a path towards their independent destiny, the person can discover a fresh outlook on life and a revitalised sense of optimism.

embracing uniqueness and independence

To weave fresh fantasies is to acknowledge each person's uniqueness and independence. Being content and joyful without relying on the love of another person is a self-evaluation and empowerment process.

Determining one's objectives and interests

In weaving new dreams, the person can discover objectives and interests that inspire and drive him. Rekindling passions and aspirations put on hold throughout the partnership might lead to fresh chances for development and self-discovery.

The efficacy of seeing the ideal future

Create fresh dreams by using a potent technique: visualising the ideal future. The person can visualise and mentally grasp his ideal life and the steps necessary to bring it to pass.

Finding untapped talents and strengths

The process of creating new dreams may reveal to the person latent skills and abilities that were not before considered. Acknowledging and honing these abilities can promote empowerment and self-assurance.

The importance of adaptability and flexibility

To weave new dreams, one must have an adaptable and open mindset in facing any obstacles and changes. Adaptability is essential for modifying plans and objectives as a person moves closer to their fulfilment. It's also important to enjoy the process.

Putting more emphasis on creating new dreams than the final product might increase one's sense of fulfilment and satisfaction. Finding joy in each journey step can provide emotional stability and motivation.

Overcoming the anxiety for the future

Dreaming of new things can make one worry about what lies ahead. It's common to be terrified of the unknown, yet overcoming this fear can lead to new experiences and opportunities in a person's life.

Using authenticity as a process guide

Being true to yourself is one of the most important aspects of creating new aspirations. Instead of attempting to live up to expectations from others, the person might look for plans and objectives that truly represent his values and passions.

The value of endurance and patience

Crafting fresh aspirations can be a gradual process requiring endurance and patience. Remembering that every action made correctly contributes to one's fulfilment is critical.

The reflection of personal development

Creating new dreams might be a chance for personal development and improvement. Every encounter and obstacle along the road presents a chance to develop personally.

The part that intrinsic motivation plays

To weave fresh dreams, one must be internally motivated. The person might find motivation within himself and develop a resolve that helps him stay committed to his objectives.

discovering direction and significance along the path

Renewing one's sense of meaning and purpose in life can be achieved through weaving new fantasies. The person can attain a deeper sense of fulfilment and happiness by looking for plans and objectives that align with their values and passions.

In summary: Crafting a unique narrative

The chance to craft new dreams allows each person to take the lead in their own narrative. It is an empowering and self-discovery process that encourages emotional independence and personal fulfilment.

By developing personal goals and aspirations, one can break away from emotional dependence and become more open to a happy and meaningful existence. Creating fresh dreams is similar to mapping out a route to a self-sufficient future in which your inner hope beams.

This chapter teaches the individual to cherish their individuality and their capacity to design a fulfilling future in which they are the only ones involved in the plans. It is an act of self-love that supports personal growth and self-esteem as one moves towards emotional fulfilment and overcoming heartbreak.

Reduction Of Anxiety And Stress

Stress and anxiety can be chronic, undesired "bonus" issues that are difficult, if not impossible, to distinguish from ADHD (attention deficit hyperactivity disorder). The inattention, impulsivity, and restlessness/hyperactivity that characterise ADHD disease can make it more difficult to complete even basic tasks at home, school, or the workplace, even if the symptoms in adults and children may look different. Stress, worry, and unpredictability can become daily companions; in fact, anxiety disorders rank among the most common co-occurring conditions among those with ADHD.

Of course, there are more intricate factors to take into account when attempting to link anxiety with ADHD. Determining whether anxiety is a sign of ADHD or if the two conditions coexist may be challenging. Whatever the case, developing coping mechanisms for handling stress and anxiety in conjunction with treating ADHD may improve the efficacy of treatment for both disorders.

Anxiety vs. ADHD

Anxiety symptoms may be similar to those of ADHD-inattentive type, formerly known as attention deficit disorder or ADD. For instance, difficulty falling asleep, feeling uncomfortable or restless, or difficulty focusing could all be signs of anxiety or ADHD. The primary distinction is what sets off the symptoms. People with ADHD are frequently distracted even in quiet settings, while those with anxiety have trouble focusing since their thoughts are so intense and unsettling.

Since people with ADHD are also more prone to suffer anxiety connected to problems originating from their mental health condition, it may not always be easy to determine the cause of troubling symptoms. Almost every part of everyday life may be significantly impacted by ADHD, and individuals who have it may be acutely aware of how they are not living up to their expectations but still struggle to modify their behaviour. These typical situations that could result from ADHD can also cause anxiety. These include failing to prioritise chores, missing instructions because you were preoccupied during a discussion, missing critical deadlines or meetings at work, and feeling awful because you upset someone you care about with an impulsive outburst.

Anxiety and ADHD symptoms can occasionally coexist, which can delay getting the right diagnosis or treatment. Before diagnosing ADHD or vice versa, a mental health expert should thoroughly analyse symptoms to rule out anxiety concerns. An efficient treatment plan must first have a clear diagnosis.

Can Stress Make ADHD Worse?

You are not dreaming if you have ever experienced difficulties controlling your ADHD when under pressure. The physiological reaction of your body to outside stimuli aggravates the common symptoms of ADHD. Stress hormones trigger a fight-or-flight response that, among other things, depletes the prefrontal cortex, which already has an impact on ADHD and regulates executive function. Working memory, mental flexibility, impulse control, coping mechanisms, and sustained attention are all hampered by the stress reaction. Even worse, extended stress may alter the brain's biochemistry and impair regular brain function. It's easy to become caught up in a vicious loop where stress exacerbates ADHD and makes people even more stressed out. Nevertheless, that tendency can be reversed with the right diagnosis and care.

Getting the help you require for ADHD, stress, and anxiety

The optimal method for treating anxiety in people with ADHD may vary depending on the individual, particularly if ADHD is the primary source of concern. Suppose you don't already have a proven diagnosis or fear it may not be accurate. In that case, we advise you to seek out assessment and testing to acquire a clearer picture, as you'll have better results if you know exactly what you're dealing with.

Behavioural therapies, medication (either stimulant or non-stimulant), and counselling are frequently used to treat ADHD. Success requires a comprehensive strategy; treatment and drugs cannot be utilised in isolation. The goal of ADHD medication is to reduce symptoms by balancing the levels of key neurotransmitters. With the use of therapy, people can modify their negative thoughts and behaviour patterns to better function and manage their symptoms of ADHD. Addressing ADHD head-on, realising that day-to-day struggles aren't personal failings but rather the result of a neurologically based illness, and developing more effective coping mechanisms can all help reduce anxiety related to ADHD and enhance the diagnosis as a whole.

If you have ADHD, changing your lifestyle may also help you better manage stress and anxiety. It's beneficial to maintain a nutritious diet, cut back on alcohol and/or caffeine, and stop smoking. Making a routine that includes exercise and breaks is also important. Learning how to relax, even with simple breathing exercises, may help you manage your stress before it becomes too much. The best results will come from consistency, so rather than making a drastic change, think about introducing these adjustments gradually so they become simple habits.

6. Mindful Social Media Use: - Use social media with awareness. Think about your intentions before using any social media platform. Restrict your social media activity and refrain from mindless scrolling to preserve a healthy balance.

7. Conscientious Prioritisation and Task Planning

The Problem: Stress and poor planning can result from excessive task lists.

The Answer is mindful task planning. Prioritise your work carefully. Rather than compiling a long list, concentrate on a reasonable amount of goals-aligned tasks. In thoughtful productivity, quality frequently wins out over quantity.

- Having Reasonable Expectations: Regard your abilities realistically. Recognise your limitations and establish reasonable goals for achieving your goals in the allotted time. Mindful planning is about letting go of pressure from within and practising self-compassion.

8. Contemplative Review at the End of the Day

The Challenge: Neglecting to take stock of the day's successes and setbacks might impede one's personal and professional advancement.

The Remedies: - Evening Conclude the day with mindfulness by engaging in mindful reflection. Spend some time at the end of each day thinking back on your successes, setbacks, and lessons discovered. This exercise improves self-awareness and lays the groundwork for ongoing development.

- Gratitude Journaling: - Include appreciation in your introspection. Think about writing down your moments of thankfulness throughout the day in a gratitude notebook. This constructive exercise strengthens an appreciation- and mindfulness-based mindset.

9. Conscious Communication

The Obstacle:

Rapid-fire communication might result in miscommunication and lost opportunities.

The Answer: - Mindful Communication Methods: - Communicate with awareness. Pay close attention and be present when conversing. Refrain from interjecting and let people have room to express themselves. Improved comprehension and connection are fostered by mindful conversation.

Digital Detox Timeframes: Set aside time for digital detoxification. Set aside daily periods to interact with people in person instead of using digital devices. This deliberate respite from screens encourages attentive communication.

10. Constant Instruction in Mindfulness

The Obstacle:

It takes practice and constant commitment to stay attentive.

The Resolution:

Constant Mindfulness Education: Spend money on mindfulness instruction. Participate in mindfulness seminars, attend workshops, or download guided meditation applications to enhance your mindfulness practice. Continuous training maintains long-term benefits and strengthens thoughtful habits.

Developing Mindful Leadership: Promote thoughtful leadership. Leaders who integrate mindfulness into their leadership style can create a mindful working culture. This entails encouraging a pleasant work environment, setting an example of mindful behaviour, and helping staff members along their mindfulness journey.

In summary, mindful productivity is an all-encompassing strategy that involves developing a presence that improves the calibre and impact of your work in addition to finishing chores. By incorporating mindfulness into your everyday practice, you may foster a focused, resilient, and well-being-promoting work atmosphere. Accept the tenets and methods of mindful productivity, understanding that the path to increased presence is ongoing and fulfilling. I hope your quest for mindful productivity results in a more purposeful and happy working life.

Honouring The Journey

We'll talk about the value of commemorating your path of self-awareness and personal development in this last chapter. You may build resilience and self-confidence by strengthening your self-esteem and laying a strong foundation for your accomplishments and advancement.

Acknowledging Your Successes:

Throughout this book, you studied self-perception, self-compassion, assertive communication, flexibility, failure-avoidance strategies, and self-improvement. Every one of these subjects aided in her quest for self-awareness and development.

Why Hold a Celebration?

There are various reasons why it's crucial to celebrate your journey:

1. Boosts Confidence in Oneself: Acknowledging your successes boosts your self-confidence by constantly reminding you of your potential and advancement.

3. Gratitude: This aids in developing an attitude of thankfulness for the encounters and knowledge life has bestowed upon you.

How to Honour Your Experience:

1. Create a list of accomplishments: Enumerate every achievement you have made on your path, no matter how tiny.

2. Honour significant anniversaries: Celebrate important milestones along the way, like a special meal, a trip, or an expression of thanks.

3. Take Stock and Express gratitude: Give yourself space to reflect on your experiences.

Exercise in Practice: A Note of Appreciation

Thank you for all the lessons you've learned and the personal development you've experienced on this journey. Write a letter to yourself.

The Trip Never Ends:

Keep in mind that self-improvement and self-discovery are lifelong endeavours. In addition to celebrating your successes, you are preparing for future trials and triumphs.

The Significance of Durable Self-Respect:

You can develop enduring self-esteem based on your capacity to overcome obstacles, gain knowledge from experiences, and keep evolving by acknowledging and appreciating your journey.

Remain Aware of Authenticity:

Stay true to yourself as you travel further. Stay true to yourself and what you stand for; a healthy sense of self-worth depends on it.

Recognition:

We appreciate you following along on this path of introspection and development. Never forget that high self-esteem gives you the resilience and confidence to tackle life's obstacles.

Honour your path, honour who you are, and keep getting better. Opportunities for development, education, and success abound in the future.

Although this book concludes, your self-awareness and personal development journey is only getting started.

Think about MalalaYousafzai, the youngest recipient of the Nobel Peace Prize in history. In a hilarious turn of events, she was called into the school office in her high school chemistry class and discovered she had won the reward. In a National Public Radio (NPR) interview, Yousafzai recalled that the teacher "usually only calls you when you're in trouble." I was thinking, "Fingers crossed!" I hope I didn't do anything incorrectly. She later informed me that I had received the Nobel Peace Prize (2023).

Yousafzai is the perfect example of genuineness. She was born in Pakistan in 1997 and developed an early love of learning. In their little hamlet, she went to a school for girls that her father ran. Speaking up for girls' access to an education in the conservative, Taliban-controlled region was her father. The Taliban government eventually started closing or demolishing female' schools. Yousafzai remained faithful to her genuine self as a child by advocating for her right to an education, even in the face of death threats from the Taliban. At eleven years old, she spoke in front of a local press club for the first time. The Taliban recognised her and began to personally attack her after she had been blogging as an activist and appearing on TV for some time. At the age of fifteen, they shot her in the face at point-blank range and left her for dead.

She somehow made it through. She later earned degrees in philosophy, politics, and economics from the prestigious Oxford University. Through her non-profit organisation, the Malala Fund, she has inspired people worldwide with her fight for girls' rights and education. Because of Yousafzai's extraordinary self-assurance, tenacity, and genuineness, she muster the bravery to alter the world and accomplish extraordinary achievements in her academic and activist work. Girls and women worldwide are loyal to their actual desires and needs.

Recognising and Eliminating Masking Behaviours

Masking is a technique that is frequently used unintentionally to shield the inner self from stressful or hazardous circumstances. This process suppresses feelings that come spontaneously and might not fit social norms. Masking is disguising one feeling with another to deflect criticism from others (Naran, 2022).

The following are examples of masking behaviours: reacting angrily or putting the blame on other people to avoid criticism or rejection; utilising humour to divert attention from an internal state of anxiety, misery, guilt, or humiliation; manufactured happiness.

These actions directly undermine any desire for authenticity and disprove self-awareness by intentionally working to bury the true self. Sometimes, masking behaviours can be so commonplace that we mistake them for our actual feelings, which causes us to become deeply estranged from our true selves. Recognising and observing the masking behaviours you may find yourself engaging in is the first step in kicking the habit of masking. This necessitates deliberate, ongoing self-reflection. Once we recognise them, we may use that self-awareness to connect with our emotions more deeply and, as a result, gain a greater understanding of our fundamental selves.

Masking behaviours can build up over time and become inauthentic identities. By now, instead of using one false emotion to mask another, you have amassed a repertoire of fake reactions, none representing your true beliefs or feelings in response to situations, social cues, or character attributes. You are seriously harming yourself if you hold onto such a false image of yourself.

Try using these methods to identify and let go of inauthentic personalities during your next self-reflection session:

Acknowledge

Notice situations or persons that may be triggers for masking behaviour. As an illustration:

You write a report, and your supervisor tells you to correct several details. You react defensively and angrily, taking this as an attack. This is a masking signal; therefore, your boss's suggestion that your work is subpar may offend you. Alternatively, perhaps you are afraid and would like to conceal your fear. You overcompensate by responding angrily.

Travel back in time to that moment.

Take yourself out of the hurt, terror, and fury states.

Recognise that your true emotions are legitimate.

Take a third-person look at the situation. Your supervisor wasn't attempting to offend or make you feel worthless. They only asked that you go over it again and improve. The fact that you were never in danger shows that the mask is superfluous.

Shed

Imagine becoming who you truly are:

Without the masks, who are you?

Who are you aspiring to be?

Is there someone you can try to emulate as a role model in your life?

Say or write a description of yourself that reflects how you want others to see you. Do you have patience, compassion, and empathy? Or maybe you're easily enraged and judgmental? Jot down the attributes you hope to be recognised for.

Face your concerns: Which underlying fears are you aware you might be hiding?

Examine the underlying reasons behind your masking or trigger behaviour. These actions frequently result from feelings of worthlessness or rejection. Recognise that those anxieties are unfounded and face them head-on.

Detach: You can successfully free yourself from the need for outside affirmation if you realise that your anxieties are unfounded.

Make an effort to accept who you are. Recognise that wearing the masks will only impede your progress towards your objectives and successes. Your genuine thoughts, emotions, and responses are essential to realising your greatest potential.

AhmadouDiallo had a colourful sense of humour. Although friends and family appreciated his ability to lighten the mood, few knew that his jokes were a mask covering an interior illness. Beneath his outward smile was a festering mass of remorse and unhappiness.

Ahmadou always had to deal with difficulties and criticism in his work life. He reacted angrily, projecting his displeasure and inadequacy onto others instead of expressing them. His conversations with his supervisor revealed a lot. He reacted defensively because he saw every suggestion or correction as an attack. His coworkersdidn't see the wounded youngster who thought his work was never good enough; they saw an angry guy. He had a similarly complicated connection with his idea of himself. In social settings, he played the part of a happy, fulfilled person, fabricating bliss. This picture was far from accurate in reality.

Ahmadou's awareness increased over time. After realising what was causing his disguising behaviour, he embarked on a self-reflection trip. His journey was not easy; it involved feelings of worthlessness and rejection. He needed to take a step back in time, examine his angry, upset, and panicked times, and discover the true nature of those emotions.

He removed his mask gradually. He was able to identify himself and his goals with the use of visualisation exercises.

Writing out the traits he wanted to have, facing his concerns, and letting go of outside approval were all crucial phases in his process. It was a difficult and in-depth growth, reflection, and unlearning process. The masks that had appeared protective turned out to be barriers that prevented him from embracing his actual thoughts and feelings. He finally felt free. Ahmadou's tale shows that we can all muster the strength to "drop the mask" and embrace authenticity, regardless of the masks we may choose to wear—religious, cultural, or emotional.

"Just dare to be yourself," he says. Don't be afraid to acknowledge that you are not alone. Accepting this fact opens the door to living a more genuine life, and the helpful suggestions in this section work as a guide through this difficult process.

Creating A Positive Attitude

Greetings and salutations from a transformative chapter in "Think Rich, Grow Rich: Building a Mindset for Wealth Creation." This chapter, "Cultivating a Wealth Mindset," takes us on a trip that goes beyond our financial goals and explores the foundation of our attitudes, beliefs, and ideas. This is where the spotlight shines on the challenging mental terrain, where belief, self-talk, and perseverance are the building blocks of success. In the following paragraphs, we explore the important ideas of breaking through limiting beliefs, encouraging positive self-talk, and developing the unwavering qualities of persistence and resilience.

Section Four

1. Getting Rid of Limiting Ideas

The path to creating riches starts in the mind, a place that is sometimes obscured by constrictive ideas that impede development. This chapter begins with breaking down the barriers of self-doubt and discussing the importance of rephrasing our ideas. By using the experiences of individuals who have overcome their obstacles as a source of inspiration, we shed light on the importance of self-awareness and its capacity to awaken the latent potential within each of us. "Cultivating a Wealth Mindset" serves as a helpful reminder that belief is the foundation upon which wealth is constructed.

2. Promoting Positive Self-Talk

Self-talk is the quiet builder of our reality, operating within the chapters of our story. The art of cultivating positive self-talk—a practice that tends to the seeds of self-worth, self-confidence, and resolve—is explored in the second section. We discover that the words we say to ourselves become the guiding lights that show us the way to financial success through stories that highlight the transformational power of self-affirmation. "Cultivating a Wealth Mindset" pushes us to develop a garden of empowering self-dialogue, where doubt withers and opportunity blooms flourish.

3. Fostering Resilience and Persistence

The obstacles we face while developing a wealth mindset put our willpower to the test. We explore the alchemy of cultivating perseverance and resilience in the third section. We look at the experiences of those who overcame obstacles, failures, and setbacks to become stronger and more determined. This chapter section shows that building money requires a symphony of commitment, grit, and steadfast drive rather than a straight path.

"Cultivating a Wealth Mindset" forces us to see every obstacle as a learning opportunity and to develop the perseverance needed to go beyond each one that stands in our way.

Section Four

We navigate the complex fabric of a wealth mindset in the following chapters. Overcoming limiting beliefs, cultivating positive self-talk, and strengthening our will and resilience pave the path to abundance that speaks to our innermost selves and financial success. Let's embrace the ideas that will shape our thoughts into rich environments where wealth, in all of its forms, can increase as we dive into this life-changing chapter.

Aid in the Self-Building of Others

I taught for my first year in Duncan, a small town in southeast Arizona. It was my job to teach 1st-grade pupils how to read. Since I had never taught before, I was not entirely confident in my abilities, but I entered the classroom with a strong passion and an unwavering love for kids.

When a pupil struggled with an assignment, I would place my hand over theirs and offer "Tomorrow." I incorporated parents in the process and built on each student's strengths as I got to know them. When a parent came in and contributed to the process in some way, from coming to observe the class to show them how their family prepares tortillas to visit farms or writing letters. Every time a child was featured, it boosted their sense of acceptance and self-worth, which kept them interested in their education.

It was an exhilarating and sometimes frightening experience, but every small victory my kids achieved gave me the courage to continue using my teaching methods. I was thinking, rearranging, shifting, and doing all the while. More success followed success. And 98% of my class was reading at a second-grade level or above by the end of the year.

Fostering self-worth in others is an admirable undertaking that can have a favourable effect on the lives of individuals in your vicinity. Observing others blossom and succeed after a little prodding from you has a wonderful effect on your self-worth and confidence. You may assist people in developing their sense of self-worth in the following ways:

★ Pay attention: Pay attention to them and attempt to comprehend their emotions and challenges. You can communicate with someone you value and care about by offering your undivided attention.

★ Compliment: Give sincere remarks and affirmations. Emphasise their accomplishments and strengths and convey your appreciation for them.

★ Motivate: Motivate people to try new things and take on difficulties. Tell them you are here to support them and that you have faith in their talents.

★ Show empathy by placing yourself in their position. It is important to affirm their experiences and acknowledge their sentiments, even if you do not entirely get what they are going through.

★Set a good example for others: Self-respect, self-care, and good self-talk. By modelling this behaviour, you may encourage children to treat themselves with love and compassion.

Talk to them about their talents, abilities, and distinctive characteristics to assist them in identifying their strengths. Urge them to concentrate on and expand upon their areas of strength.

★ Assist: Be there for them when they require assistance, direction, or a sympathetic ear. Tell them you are available to them and that they can rely on you.

Remember that developing self-esteem is a long process that requires patience and work. You may assist someone in developing their sense of self-worth and becoming the best version of themselves by providing your encouragement and support.

These are only a few tried-and-true strategies for boosting one's own and other people's self-esteem. Plenty of alternative solutions are available if one doesn't suit your needs. Continue to learn, develop, and expand your expertise in this field at all times.

Remember to be kind to yourself if it takes a while to notice the benefits. Do not worry if you are unsure about where to begin! We're going to concentrate on it now!

Think and Take Action

Which of these tactics struck a chord with you?

Select one and work through the steps to incorporate it into your everyday routine.

After working on it for a week, tell a reliable buddy about your experience.

● "I made a mistake, but I can improve."

That's alright. I am aware of my errors. I'm not the only one that does that, either. What counts is how I proceed.

● "All right! That's not a problem; I might need someone to help me learn this. I can quickly catch up once I

How much self-compassion do you possess? In the following chapter, we'll discuss measuring and tracking self-compassion.

Think and Take Action

After reading this chapter, what are your feelings towards self-compassion?

Take a friend for a stroll and discuss your thoughts and feelings about attempting to practise self-compassion more.

Encourage them to talk about their experiences and hardships as well.

Why Does Self-Compassion Seem Difficult for Some People?

Self-compassion can be challenging for some people for a variety of reasons. Here are some potential causes:

Traditions

Many nations and cultures highly value individual success, self-discipline, and self-criticism. This may result in a propensity for harsh and critical self-criticism. Also, it could cause someone to see self-compassion as a sign of frailty or self-interest.

Let's say that mental health concerns are stigmatised in a person's culture. In that situation, people could feel embarrassed or ashamed to ask for help for their mental health problems, particularly if their culture perceives it. Feelings of worthlessness, loneliness, and hopelessness may result from this.

If they go through a mental health crisis, this can be an especially difficult circumstance for them since they can be reluctant to ask for assistance or to ask their community for support.

Early life experiences

Neglect, abuse, and criticism from carers throughout your early years might have a long-lasting effect on your capacity to treat yourself with kindness. If your childhood requirements for affection, attention, encouragement, and affirmation were not fulfilled, you may find it difficult to provide yourself with these things as an adult.

negative dialogue with oneself

Being self-compassionate might be challenging because of the negative and criticising voice of the inner critic.

Cultural messaging, early life events, or other elements may strengthen this self-defeating dialogue.

The things we hear and go through as children and important life events like the first year of marriage mould our inner critic, which is usually negative. Some of those remarks aren't even malicious; occasionally, well-meaning parents, teachers, or carers say something without realising the long-term effects.

● "Boys with strength never cry or grumble." claimed to protect the child from being harassed and abused for having strong emotions. However, it educates kids that expressing their feelings in public is inappropriate and embarrassing.

"Good girls don't fight." It teaches the youngster that their opinions and boundaries don't matter, even if it instils respect and maintains some degree of harmony in the home.

"What prevents you from being more like your brother?" This method of asking can make the child feel inadequate, even while it might be done out of frustration or to provide a reference point for an ideal role model. Their sense of self is lowered as a result.

● "You seem like an odd child." Though it can be interpreted as a loving gesture, some kids find the remark more upsetting than others. Because the word "strange" can suggest that a youngster doesn't fit in or is negatively different from their peers, it can give them the impression that they are abnormal.

● "You're starting to gain some weight." Would you mind going outside to play? Even when the long-term health of the child is considered, this can have a disastrous effect on their sense of self-worth and body image.

"Although it's an enjoyable pastime, you should prioritise a real job." When parents criticise their child's professional goals, the youngster may start to believe that they are unworthy of success or inadequate, which can negatively affect their general well-being. Their inner critic tells them, "I am not good enough to make a living doing this," rather than, "I am worthy of succeeding at this."

● "Just go ahead and do it. They are related. Although striving to foster family peace is a wonderful idea, this approach teaches the youngsters that their discomfort and boundaries are unjustified. This might cause individuals to bury their needs in favour of others, which can damage their self-esteem and self-compassion and result in issues with assertiveness and setting boundaries with others later in life.

Now, I want to ask you to wrap up in a nice blanket, sit in your favourite seat, and think about the outlook on life you have allowed yourself to have throughout the years you have lived until now. These five questions will direct your reflection so that it is precise:

What brings me daily misery?

Why does that item or person have the ability to rob me of my happiness and peace of mind?

How can I improve my judgement and view the world in a more upbeat light?

What actions and words can I take to alter the mindset I've been having towards people, myself, and life in general?

How would that look if I were to start living my life from now on with a different culture and mindset?

Since we have already discussed shedding light on self-discovery, completing this exercise, who you are and what steps you need to take to begin living a more wonderful and wise life.

We've also talked about how crucial it is that you take the lead in establishing a strong, transformative culture for both you and everyone around you. The next part contains some advice on how to get your revolution started.

Doable Daily Routines to Develop a Positive Attitude

Your customs reveal your cultural background, and conscientious and refined behaviour can make you exceptional. Let's talk about ways to start acting out so that you may support the development of a culture that values self-love, kindness, compassion, positivism, and encouragement.

Changing the way you think about success: Your paradigm is the way you choose to understand the world, how you interpret events, and the predetermined perspective you hold about it, other people, and yourself. Reframing your mentality involves controlling your thoughts and preventing them from automatically identifying your events. No matter how many negative thoughts try to consume you, you actively allow them to go if they don't benefit you and instead surround yourself with more enlightening and positive ideas. This enables you to remain strong and forward-thinking even in the face of extreme adversity.

Disconnecting from self-defeating thoughts: We already know that the negative chatter that can run wild in people's minds nearly every hour can be much more piercing than the nasty, careless, and disrespectful things people say to you. This chatter can paralyse your ability to successfully develop your goals, acting like a poisonous mental programme. It does not turn off by itself, nor does wanting it to stop cause it to do so. You must intentionally remove those negative thoughts from your mind and replace them with good ones. Avoid spending too much time listening to bad news or letting those who say bad things say whatever they want whenever they feel like it. There are two ways to go about doing this. Setting and maintaining boundaries can help you say no to things that don't advance you and encourage others to be careful with their words around you.

Read uplifting, well-written novels to nourish your intellect. Reading opens your eyes to fresh ideas and viewpoints you may not have encountered. Even if reading isn't your thing, you may still fill your head with fresh concepts that will improve your performance in life. You can read an audiobook, go on a tour of the city, visit a gallery, take an online course, join a book club, take up a new sport, meet new people who are outside of your normal comfort zone, watch a talk show, or sign up for an interest-based personal development coaching programme are just a few of the many inventive ways you can do this. You may develop a culture of continuous learning that will enable you to gain wisdom and abilities to help you become the best version of yourself you could ever want.

Look for opportunities to improve and add value to the lives of others: Have you ever observed what attracts people to a particular someone and makes them want to spend a lot of money with them? It's definitely due to the worth that individual adds to the lives of others. Individuals who strive to positively impact others' lives in addition to their own are living lives of higher meaning. Because of their service, these individuals are revered and admired. Take steps to improve and beautify the world around you if you want to be a person of greater distinction and class than you have ever been.

When obstacles threaten to cause you to lose trust in your ambitions, resist the urge to falter or give up. Nearly everyone makes resolutions for the next year, full of bright prospects and limitless potential, at some point each year. The early months are typically when most people are excited and determined to change their performance in the coming year. But as time goes on, what typically occurs? Desperation and complacency set very swiftly. Aspirations you once fervently believed in become unachievable due to hopelessness and unbelief. Before quickly, you start settling for far less than you know you can, and your plans abruptly change. When obstacles and difficulties are blowing through your life, it's a good idea to give up on your aspirations. This annual habit of giving up on dreams may not seem to be a huge concern; nonetheless, it truly is. This is because, depending on how much you tolerate it, the trajectory of your entire life may very rapidly begin to take this substandard track. The temptation to adopt this mindset and culture can be very strong when you're young and witness your friends look unfazed by the idea of accomplishing their goals.

The Thing We Refer To As Emotions

Hi, how are you feeling right now?

How often do we pose this query to ourselves? How frequently do we pose this query to other people?

The latter is the more straightforward choice, and we hardly ever take the time to consider how we are feeling.

Can you accurately identify your current emotional state even if you ask yourself that question?

- Are you content?
- ✓ Depressed?
- ✓ Feeling overwhelmed?
- Angry?
- Uneasy?
- Excited?

✏ Fearful?

✓ What if you experienced multiple feelings simultaneously?

✏ What does it mean to feel all these emotions?

✏ From where does it originate?

✏ What causes our feelings to be the same?

Emotions is just one word, but it raises so many questions.

Are Feelings and Emotions the Same Thing?

Yes, most would agree; feelings and emotions are the same. Still, that's not true. Though they could have a similar feel, emotions are very different experiences. They are distinct entities even if they occasionally rely on one another. Emotions are defined as the subconsciously produced physiological state we experience. Our bodies' natural reaction to internal or external stimuli that cause this reaction is known as an emotion. When you experience an emotion, it is frequently aimed towards something, someone, or a past event.

There is a purpose behind your feelings of terror. Your experience, something you've encountered, or someone else caused you to feel that way.

Contrarily, feelings are irrational and shaped by our conscious and reflective thinking. This suggests that although feelings are not necessary for emotions to exist, they cannot exist without feelings.

Alright, What Exactly Are Feelings?

The best way to characterise emotions is to define them as strong feelings you have towards situations, whether they are imagined or actual. This is your brain's way of alerting you to something that has been noticed in your surroundings. Your body will release the corresponding emotional reaction in response to that trigger.

Put another way; your brain starts working when something happens in your surroundings and tries to make sense of it. Your body enters the fight-or-flight reaction mode, and that stimulus is interpreted as a threat. Emotions such as fear, anxiety, and occasionally even fury follow. After that, you'll have to decide between two possibilities. You can either run away from your fear or maintain your ground.

A new set of hormones floods your system when your brain interprets the trigger as favourable. The feel-good chemicals oxytocin, dopamine, and serotonin are in charge of feelings like joy, enthusiasm, excitement, curiosity, and even arousal. You're far more likely to stay in these situations because you like the feelings you're experiencing rather than giving in to the need to run away.

Part of the reason humans have lasted this long is because of our emotional experiences and reactions. They are essential to the development of the human race as a whole. As long as humans have lived on this earth, our emotions have taught us how to conceal, hunt, battle, socialise, and even procreate. Emotions were much easier to define when our surroundings were simpler than now. These days, anything can potentially set off a strong emotion. One such trigger could be social media. One's job may act as a trigger. Managing the obligations of family life may also act as a trigger. Even the pressure to meet the irrational standards of perfection set by society can set off a cascade of powerful emotions.

Emotions are erratic; they are always shifting based on our circumstances and the things that set off particular reactions in us. When strong emotions are involved, reason and logic are abandoned. How often have you let an intense emotional episode get the better of you and then acted rashly in a way you later regretted? Maybe more often than you'd want to admit, perhaps too frequently.

The contemporary environment is ever-evolving. As a result of these adjustments, you may. Your emotions, their meanings, and your ability to control them can help you start the process of becoming an emotional intelligence.

Recognising Our Basic Human Feelings

Though we can feel a wide variety of emotions known by many different names, our fundamental emotions may be categorised into seven things:

Joy (happiness)

Startled

dread disgust

Disregard

Fury

Sadness

Picture Credit: emotions

The other emotions are constructed on top of these seven fundamental emotions. According to experts, humans may experience up to 25 secondary emotions.

The interesting thing about emotions is that they usually happen subconsciously.

This implies that you can be exhibiting symptoms of strong emotions without even realising it. Consider a situation where you're viewing a scary movie alone at home to demonstrate this idea. You are aware that you are at home and in a secure setting. You understand this is just a movie; thus, nothing can harm you here. However, as the film goes on, you start to feel anxious, irritated, and perhaps even a little jittery or afraid. Despite these feelings, you're still intrigued by the film and want to see what happens next. Your heart rate rises in response to your body's feelings. You may even notice that your palms are sweaty and chilly, and your pupils are dilated in terror. Your body's autonomous system functions before you can even start consciously processing your emotions.

Picture Credit: emotions

Of course, the Two-Factor Theory was also criticised; these generally came from research showing how emotions could be controlled even when a person could not cognitively explain the stimuli.

In one such study, Robert Zajonc and William Kunst-Wilson discovered that although the participants in their research could not correctly identify the stimuli, this did not prevent them from developing affective discriminations.

Chapter 6 Mastering the Art of "No"

Learning to say "no" is essential for anyone trying to break free from codependency and establish strong boundaries in relationships. Codependents frequently struggle with a tendency to put their own needs ahead of those of others, as well as a constant sense of guilt and a fear of rejection. In the following pages, we'll explore the critical importance of saying "no," impart the knowledge of assertiveness training, and provide techniques for overcoming the shame and anxiety frequently associated with setting limits and declining requests.

The Significance of Saying "No"

Speaking "no" is fundamental to maintaining healthy boundaries and developing self-worth. It doesn't indicate a lack of collaboration or encouragement. Instead, it emphasises stating one's wants, defining one's boundaries, and placing one's values first. The following are some strong justifications for saying "no":

1. Self-Respect: Saying "no" expresses self-respect and self-worth. It emphasises the importance of one's

welfare and offers a tangible confirmation of one's limits and values.

2. Equilibrium in Relationships: Mutual respect and equilibrium are essential to healthy relationships. Saying "no" when the situation demands it aids in striking this give-and-take equilibrium.

3. Preventing Resentment: Codependents often build up a festering resentment by giving their consent with a "yes" when they truly mean to say "no." The development of the ability to say "no" prevents this build-up of hidden annoyance and psychological stress.

4. Promoting Self-Empowerment: Saying "no" can be a powerful way to gain empowerment. It gives someone the confidence to express their demands and make decisions. This empowerment then contributes to an increase in confidence and self-worth.

Instruction in Self-Assertion

Being able to say "no" while maintaining the integrity of relationships requires mastering the art of assertiveness, which is communicating one's needs, wants, and feelings courteously and directly. The following are some methods for developing assertiveness:

First, make use of "I" statements. Rather than saying, "You make me feel overwhelmed," think about saying, "I feel overwhelmed when my responsibilities become overwhelming." Using "I" phrases shifts the emphasis on the subject's feelings and experiences, which reduces the likelihood of an accusing impression.

2. Choose Clear and Direct Communication: Use concise language to convey your decision to turn down an offer or set limits. It is best to avoid

using vague or ambiguous wording as it could lead to miscommunication.

3. Keep Eye Contact: It's important to keep adequate eye contact when engaging in encounters that call for assertiveness. It exudes confidence and genuineness at the same time.

4. Practice Active Listening: Paying attention to what the other person has to say shows that you are receptive to their point of view. In the conversation, this fosters respect for one another.

5. Project Calm and Composure: Retain your emotional composure when you answer "no." Refrain from escalating into hostility, defensiveness, or excessive emotional display.

6. Use Nonverbal Cues: Body language and voice intonation are important nonverbal cues. They function as components of nonverbal

communication that need close examination. A calm tone, assertive body language, and an open and non-threatening stance can support the message's air of respect and assertiveness.

7. Initial Practice: Make it a habit to practice forceful responses before you engage in real-life situations that require assertiveness. Role-playing with a trustworthy friend or therapist lays the groundwork for developing self-assurance.

How To Encourage Conversations With Those Around You

You pull into the parking lot, turn off the car, take a seat, and for a minute, you sit there dreading the next two hours. An important client has invited you to an open house to celebrate the opening of their new downtown office. You don't like things like that. You feel like you're not trying to look lost, so you eat and drink more than you should to keep occupied. Other than the customer, you have no idea what to do. You don't know anybody. You must attend, yet you slump into the front seat and wring your hands over how long you must stay. If you're not staying for the entire event, will you upset one of your biggest clients or drop the trick for thirty minutes? You're trying to figure out how to leave as soon as possible. At a predetermined moment, someone might message you with a purported emergency; perhaps one of the kids has a major game, or perhaps you'll just allow your dread to lead you straight into a medical condition.

At least twelve occasions a day are spent in casual conversation: driving to work, picking up your daughter from soccer practice, taking the lift with a friend, making a phone call to your mother-in-law, going to a business conference, having lunch with a client, attending a job interview — the list is endless! However, these demands for small conversations don't simplify things for some of us. These encounters, if anything, create anxiety and encourage certain people to avoid social events, business lunches, and chance neighbour experiences. Sadly, people close to us—friends, acquaintances, and associates—

see us as aloof, frigid, and guarded regarding our difficulties.

You're at the right place if you find that your conversations end almost as soon as they begin or if you avoid social and professional gatherings. The book will assist you in gaining the communication skills necessary to feel confident and at ease in any circumstance. You to banish your conversational demons.

3.1 Small Conversation

Small chat has a poor reputation as the ugly stepchild of meaningful discourse, but it has a vital function. You rarely get to the real subject without it. Small talk serves as the icebreaker, opening the door to a more intimate conversation and strengthening your bond. Individuals skilled in small talk are masters at creating a welcoming, respectful, and easygoing atmosphere for others. And it helps to build a commercial relationship, negotiate a contract, establish a friendship, or simply have a friend. The benefit of conversational skills is that anyone may become proficient in them. Don't let someone fool you into thinking that it comes effortlessly to them since so many other people laugh and interact with joy. While some are fluent in the language, most had to practise. They have been reading books, finding personal mentors, attending workshops, and practising. I became an expert by picking up and using my abilities, which is simple.

The first step is to give up the idea that everyone should be able to communicate with strangers and friends. It's just not real, this. Neither is a biological mechanism that kicks in when we encounter a conversational impasse; we are not taught how to do it. Many people, including fairly positive socialites, find small conversations difficult. It's much simpler for small conversation than you imagine, so let's blow through these.

3.2 Tips for Getting Better at Small Talk

More skills are needed to be proficient in small chat than in any other discussion area. In particular, the time constraint allows you to influence others and consciously or unconsciously draw them into a longer discussion. Thus, the following advice is applicable in a variety of circumstances.

One Question: You are limited to asking one question at a time. You have to replace a question with something else after you have one. Try rephrasing your query as an argument. "What are you doing for work?" It is "Extremely hard work is required.

We say exceedingly brief stories in small chats or short-sentence stories. The day before I did my plane jump, I tried my hand at stand-up comedy and failed. Of the two, I believe being the centre of attention for a hundred people for two minutes was a bit more unsettling. You can begin if someone requests further information. If not, perhaps you could concentrate on your previews.

Tell Me More: When asked a story, the best response is always "tell me more." Select and go deeper into the storyline that most piqued your attention. Conversely, the worst reaction to a story is, "Let me tell you how well I did that."

Make a mistake—you are not required to respond to the party's query. It's not even required of you to respond to all of the questions posed to you. "What do you do for work?" "I'm trying to sell a business. What are you doing?" Ignoring the problem of corporate sales? What does it signify, as I've never heard of it before? People are not used to being acknowledged, especially when it implies that someone else is giving up their speaking opportunity. They will ask again at the end of the day if they truly need your response.

Turn it up a notch: Tailor your discourse to the individuals' degree of intensity when they adopt the same manner and are reasonably calm and self-assured. However, after that, inject a tiny bit of vigour by being there during the discussion.

People will adjust to your energy level and become slightly more animated during the conversation. It accomplishes two things. Firstly, you take on the role of defector operator, assisting you in steering the conversation towards interesting subjects. Secondly, when individuals break free from their typical conversational patterns, they become more involved and finally make their own decisions on communication, which improves the environment for everyone.

Regarding Advice in Small Talk: Small Talk is a joke. If someone asks you for advice, you don't provide it. "How did you meet so many individuals? You no longer engage in small talk; offer it if they keep going. Generally speaking, don't advise in any case unless you've already kind of objected to it, and they've gone on.

Chapter 10: Visualization for Happiness, Love, and Achievement with Affirmation Alchemy

Introduction

"You are not outside of the cosmos. Examine yourself; you already own all you desire." - Rumi.

Hi there! You are about to embark on an incredible journey, and I am honoured to accompany you. You have a guide, or maybe it's on your screen. A kind of road map intended to help you unleash the universe's vast, limitless, and frequently unrealized energy and create a life-changing shift.

Although it may seem too magical or fantastical to be true, this is based on the principles of quantum physics. The fundamental component of our life is energy, and our thoughts and emotions are strong energy sources. They produce vibrations that influence our reality by interacting with the universe's energy.

I'd like you to take the time to consider your own life now. Have you ever observed how some patterns consistently recur? How does it appear like bad things happen more often when you're depressed? Or how easy excellent things come when you have an optimistic outlook? This is the Law of Universal Attraction in operation, not just a coincidence.

releasing the inner power

Understanding this basic idea is similar to receiving the key to open the door to a different universe. We may deliberately cultivate optimism and align ourselves with the frequencies that attract what we seek by becoming aware of the power of our thoughts and emotions.

Consider yourself as a radio station listener. You must adjust your dial to the frequency at which the station you want to listen to is broadcasting because each station has a distinct frequency. The Law of Universal Attraction works similarly. We must get better at directing our feelings and ideas towards the frequencies corresponding to our goals.

However, how can we go about doing this? How can we change our perspective from one of scarcity and negativity to one of plenty and optimism? This is the real beginning of the process of self-discovery and development.

Accepting the enchantment of materialization

The art of manifesting uses the Law of Universal Attraction to consciously create the life we want. It involves actively co-creating our reality with the universe rather than passively hoping for something to happen.

We must clearly and firmly picture our goals before bringing them to life on canvas, just as an artist does. The magic is in this place by sending out vibrations that align with them when we mix our thoughts with the heightened feelings of pleasure, appreciation, and love.

However, manifestation is an ongoing process rather than an isolated incident. It calls for endurance, patience, and faith in the universe. To completely embrace the power of the Law of Universal Attraction, we must recognize and let go of any limiting ideas or unfavourable patterns. This requires self-reflection and self-awareness.

Are you prepared to harness the power of the Law of Universal Attraction, my fellow truth-seeker? Are you prepared to take on the responsibilities of a deliberate co-creator of your life? Fasten your seatbelts; the voyage ahead is full of life-changing opportunities. Let's go on this journey together, hand in hand, and discover the magic each of us possesses.

We frequently undervalue the influence that our thoughts and feelings have. However, the reality is that they have amazing power to influence our reality and draw in the situations we want. This is what the Law of Universal Attraction is all about. When we comprehend and accept this truth, we can learn to synchronize our thoughts and feelings with the frequencies that attract what we truly want.

We must become aware of the energy we are releasing into the cosmos if we are to properly utilize the Law of Universal Attraction. We attract specific things into our lives based on the vibration of our thoughts. We must learn to synchronize our thoughts and emotions with our desired manifestations, like adjusting the radio to the correct frequency.

Think of yourself as a magnet drawing everything with the same vibrational frequency. You will attract situations and chances consistent with your prevailing beliefs when you send signals into the cosmos. This is why thinking of empowering and positive ideas is crucial despite obstacles. You generate a magnetic pull towards success and optimism by doing this.

That being said, bringing our ideas and feelings to our desires is not always simple. Since we are all human, it is normal for us to occasionally have bad feelings and thoughts. The secret is recognizing these harmful tendencies and deliberately changing them to more powerful and beneficial ones. You can rewire your thinking to attract more of what you want, but it may take some time and practice.

Visualization is highly effective for bringing your thoughts and feelings into harmony with the frequencies that draw in the things you want. You can harness the power of your imagination by visualizing in detail what you wish to materialize. You draw that desired reality closer to yourself with every thought and feeling when you can see, feel, and believe in it.

Gratitude is a vital habit in line with the Law of Universal Attraction. You can become more receptive to blessings and elevate your vibration by expressing thanks for what you already have. Concentrating on its positive features can attract more optimism into your life.

Remember that the Law of Universal Attraction is always in effect whether we are conscious of it or not. Unleashing the magic within us, we may create a reality full of pleasure, love, and success by learning to align our thoughts and emotions with the frequencies that attract our dreams. So embrace your ability to choose your future and let go of any constraints or uncertainties. The universe is waiting to align with your desires, so get ready to manifest the life of your dreams.

Find doable tactics to change your reality and attract favourable conditions.

We learn more about the Law of Universal Attraction and realize that it involves more than just feeling and thinking positively. It all comes down to directing our feelings and ideas towards the frequencies that draw the things we want. It involves entering a state of consciousness where our vibration and energy are balanced with the cosmos.

3. Why Timing Is Important

Time is a crucial component in negotiation that is frequently disregarded. Its subtle and significant impact influences attitudes, tactics, and results. As they say in olden times, "There is a time for everything," in negotiations, timing can be the very thing that makes or breaks a deal. This section explains the dance of timing, its complex meaning, and methods to fully utilize it.

3.1. Time as a Strategic Instrument

Timing is more than just chronological in the ups and downs of negotiation; it's strategic. The timing of proposal introductions, compromises, and even conversation pauses can affect how the negotiations proceed and turn out.

3.2. Important Aspects Affected by Timing

- First Impressions: The tone of the negotiation is established early on. The tone and course of the negotiation can be set early on by making strong points or exhibiting flexibility.

-Momentum: How quickly or slowly a discussion moves along influences participation and the ability to make decisions. Momentum that is well-timed might inspire enthusiasm or provide an opportunity for introspection.

-Concessions: Timing concessions can convey various emotions, including confidence, desperation, excitement, and goodwill, which can impact leverage and perceived value.

-Closure: The conditions and degree of satisfaction of all parties concerned can be affected by when to press for a contract or complete it.

3.3. Techniques for Timing Well—

Reading the Room: Develop the capacity to determine the other person's emotional and psychological state. This makes it possible for prompt interventions, such as stating a point, offering a compromise, or recommending a pause.

-The Power of Pauses: Acknowledge the influence that quiet may have. Following a suggestion, a strategic pause might force the other side to consider, react, or even give in.

-Prepare for Deadlines: Strategic advantages can arise from being aware of outside time constraints, such as fiscal year-ends or event dates.

-The Final Receipt: Late in the negotiation, especially when it comes as a surprise, making a concession might help bring the matter to a successful conclusion.

-Delays in Strategy: Although excessive use can be harmful, sometimes holding out on decisions or replies can indicate thought, boost perceived worth, or pique curiosity.

Section 7: Steer clear of overconfidence

The interviewers ask John, "Why should we choose you and not the others?" He immediately responds, "I believe I can do it better. In college, I excelled academically because I always strived to give it my all.

John speaks from personal experience and exudes confidence. The judges did not select him even though he possessed the necessary abilities for the position. You ask, but why? The reason is that John comes out as overconfident.

Being overconfident in oneself is a common mistake people make because they mistakenly believe it to be mere confidence. Fear that you might be acting similarly? Confidence and overconfidence in oneself and strategies for handling the latter at work.

Self-assurance versus overconfidence

Overconfidence and confidence are frequently confused, yet they are essentially the same thing. When we are certain that our actions are correct, we are said to be confident. We believe we are capable of doing anything, and we have faith in ourselves.

Conversely, overconfidence occurs when we place too much trust in our abilities and fail to acknowledge the possibility of error. It stems from insecurity; we try to mask our doubts by being overconfident.

Overconfidence frequently results in cockiness and poor decision-making.

Several indicators can be used to distinguish between an overconfident individual and someone confident:

Confident Personality

You have nothing to demonstrate.

You don't want others to listen to or agree with you.

You don't hesitate to speak the truth.

When you display bravery, others are forced to pay attention.

You Stay True To Who You Are

Overly proud personality

You prefer to speak than to listen.

You wish to prove your argument to them.

You are unable to acknowledge your shortcomings or faults.

You're not always who you are when you're around other people.

The overconfidence effect, a well-known defect that leads us to believe we know more and can anticipate outcomes more accurately than we actually can, is caused by overconfidence. For instance, companies enter highly competitive markets with little prospect of success.

Consequences of Overconfidence in Work

crucial, particularly if you hope to succeed at work and forge relationships with other professionals. You're more prone to dominate group discussions if you exude confidence. You won't be receptive to alternative viewpoints, which can cause arguments and altercations. When someone has too much confidence in himself, the following occurs at work:

It all comes down to the belief that you are superior to others. You're prepared to take unnecessary risks to bolster your argument.

You have a sense of control over everything. If you're in the investment business, it's particularly problematic since you tend to overestimate situations and lose sight of their level of risk.

You don't allow enough time for yourself to complete tasks. You may put things off and miss your deadlines.

How to Avoid Being Overconfident in Yourself

It is difficult for people to admit when they are overconfident in themselves. The following advice will help you avoid being overconfident in yourself:

Tell the truth to yourself.

Start by being true to yourself and putting other people's opinions and feelings about you aside. Overconfidence is the result of nervousness and self-doubt. You have to love and accept who you are. Learn what you can do, and don't hesitate to decline requests.

Stop comparing.

At school and work, we've been trained to do better than our peers. It is difficult to feel joy for others' victories when you always compare yourself to them. Instead, set your guidelines about what it means to be successful.

Let Criticism In

A lot of individuals tend to take critiques to heart. If you are sure of yourself, you will take the criticism seriously. After thinking about yourself, you'll take the steps to make those changes happen.

Listen to what other people have to say with an open mind. Listen to them!

No One Ever Stops Learning

A person who is sure of themselves never stops learning. You don't mind making mistakes or admitting when you've done something wrong. You can turn mistakes into chances to learn and work on getting better. You're not afraid to admit when you're wrong, and you're willing to look at things from another point of view.

Slow Down A person who is too sure of themselves is always eager to prove their point, so they jump to conclusions and make quick choices. A person with confidence will slow down. You won't just take things for granted anymore. Instead, you'll think about what's happening before jumping to assumptions. You won't take shortcuts, and you won't make choices on the spot.

Even though these self-help tips are helpful, the only way to stop being overconfident is to think about yourself and look inside. The Interpreting Self course from Harappa Education will teach you how to become more self-aware. The River of Life Framework will help you think about events that have changed your life. Know and admit your skills and flaws to keep yourself from getting too confident.

We dispel rumours and myths.

Various myths, stories, and misconceptions frequently surround the practice of hypnosis. These false beliefs may result from disinformation, inaccurate information, or misrepresentations.

One of the most widespread misunderstandings is the assumption that under hypnosis, you lose control of your mind and actions. In actuality, a person under hypnosis always retains control over his ideas and actions, and he cannot be coerced into acting against his moral convictions or will.

It's critical to realize that hypnosis differs from deep sleep or oblivion. The patient stays conscious and can react to the hypnotherapist's instructions and recommendations.

Hypnosis does not provide remarkable skills, nor does the hypnotherapist possess any magical powers. Instead, it's a naturally occurring mental state that can be generated with certain methods.

One of the main worries is that hypnosis increases a person's susceptibility to manipulation. In actuality, even in a trance, a person retains some level of discernment and is unlikely to act in a way inconsistent with their morals.

It is a myth that hypnosis can restore exact and comprehensive memories. Suggestions and the formation of fictitious or twisted memories are both influenced by hypnosis.

Hypnosis is generally safe when performed correctly by qualified practitioners. However, hazards, including the creation of false memories or the impression of losing mental control, could occur if they are used improperly or by non-experts.

While it is true that some persons are more prone to hypnosis than others, this does not exclude them from reaping the benefits of the technique. The patient's motivation and the hypnotherapist's abilities determine how successful hypnosis is.

If there are no alterations in the person's thoughts and actions, the effects of hypnosis may be transient or brief.

Seek information from reputable sources and, if interested, see a licensed hypnotherapist to dispel these myths and obtain a more accurate understanding of hypnosis. When used properly, hypnosis is a safe, effective method for enhancing mental and emotional health.

Hypnosis can be a useful technique for overcoming emotional obstacles and improving undesirable behaviours by influencing the subconscious mind. This technique is predicated on the notion that the subconscious mind governs a significant portion of our actions, routines, and emotional responses.

Accessing this mind during a hypnotic trance is feasible to effect good change.

Understanding the subconscious mind and the power of suggestion is the cornerstone of hypnosis.

The human mind has two distinct parts: the conscious and the subconscious. While the subconscious mind stores memories of the past, analyzes information at a deeper level and controls automatic behaviours, the conscious mind makes logical judgments and maintains day-to-day awareness.

The foundation of hypnosis is the idea that when in a hypnotic trance, the subconscious mind is extremely receptive to suggestions. Our level of awareness changes during this trance, opening up the subconscious mind to outside influences. These factors can be employed to overcome emotional obstacles, stop unhealthy habits, and alter unfavourable attitudes.

The hypnotherapist or the patient (if self-hypnotizing) induces a trance-like condition in the mind during a hypnosis session. The person becomes less receptive to outside influences and concentrates more on himself when they are in this state. By maintaining an inward focus, you can access the subconscious and present ideas that may assist in reframing your behaviour and mental processes.

For instance, a hypnotherapist may offer ideas to help someone who wants to stop smoking become more determined and willing to do so. These recommendations can support the development of new habits by guiding the subconscious mind toward a constructive objective.

Hypnosis is also useful for getting past trauma or emotional obstacles. Greater knowledge and the release of pent-up emotions are frequently the results of an individual exploring and reworking old events while in a trance.

To put it briefly, hypnosis uses the subconscious mind's innate propensity to open up to suggestions while in a trance to effect beneficial changes in feelings, ideas, and actions. This therapy approach can effectively address numerous issues, but it is crucial.

The Benefits Of Having Positive Dialogues With Yourself

The individual is one of the most potent forces in life that may be used to one's advantage. We may employ our ideas in particular since they affect our moods and, thus, have the power to significantly influence how we live our lives overall. By learning how to exercise self-talk control and replace negative self-talk—something most people do unconsciously throughout the day—with positive self-talk, you can start to take more control over every aspect of your life and make the necessary changes.

A person with a positive outlook is more assured and ultimately successful than one who is full of negativity, which breeds insecurity and poor self-worth. The way you handle life will determine how successful you are in it. A person with a positive outlook is more self-assured and eventually more successful. Positivity makes it easier to perceive the good in other people and the world, which breeds optimism and success. Your perspective on life will change when you have a negative attitude instead of a positive one. Your life's quality is determined by the thoughts and feelings you experience at any time. Modifying your thought process can profoundly affect how you perceive and react to life.

A person who approaches life with optimism and an optimistic outlook is better equipped to handle life and the challenges it occasionally presents; they can overcome obstacles and disappointments and are generally better prepared to handle life. When a person adopts this upbeat outlook on life, they can fully manage their emotions and thoughts and may even transform a bad situation by changing their perspective. The upbeat individual will perceive the issue for what it is—a transient obstacle they can overcome and move on from. When one adopts this cheery outlook on life, one will recognize the issue for what it is—a transient obstacle. Choosing positive thoughts will keep your moods, thoughts, and actions upbeat since thoughts may be either good or negative, and you can only have one notion in your mind at a time. This will make you happier and more likely to achieve your goals.

keeping a daily, positive conversation going with oneself

It will likely take some time to break the negative thought habit you have carried for a long time. Initially, repeat encouraging words to yourself about fifty times a day. Positive affirmations can be spoken out or softly to yourself to achieve this. Using constructive self-talk is one strategy for creating a new thought pattern. Positive self-talk can assist you with a wide range of aspects of your life, including conquering difficult circumstances, developing self-confidence, helping you break bad habits, getting better faster from illnesses, and improving your quality of life. The following are some typical expressions and statements that might be utilized in constructive self-talk:

● I have an interesting challenge facing me – instead of looking at the situation negatively and thinking that.

● I am facing an interesting challenge – this could be used when there is some difficulty.

● I like who I am as a person. Using this statement will help you become more confident and accept who you are. These statements are comparable to "I am the best," "I am a good person," and "I have many wonderful attributes."

The phrase "I know I can do this" might be a helpful strategy when faced with a difficulty you previously doubted your ability to complete. Another option is to say something like, "I can do this" or "This doesn't present a challenge for me."

● You can use this affirmation to promote optimistic thoughts about your health while recovering from an illness or following a medical episode.

● This affirmation, "I am full of health, energy, and vitality," can help you feel good about your physical wellbeing.

● I've realized my potential – this affirmation can be a source of good, all-encompassing thoughts about your life and the world around you.

Guide for Readers

Thank you for joining us on this insightful trip through "Mastering the Right Attitude: A Guide to Success and Happiness." This reader's guide is intended to give you a road map for efficiently interacting with the book, maximizing the insights it gives, and using those insights in your daily life.

1. Attitude Is Everything:

Before exploring the chapters, it is important to understand the book's main concept, the power of attitude. Your attitude affects how you see and react to the environment, which in turn affects your life's experiences, connections, and results. To get the most out of this tutorial, accept that you can change your mindset to achieve success and happiness.

2. Examining the Sections:

"Mastering the Right Attitude" is divided into twelve chapters, each focusing on a different facet of attitude and how it affects your life. Below is a synopsis of the contents of each chapter:

- Understanding Attitude: Learn about the fundamentals of attitude, how it develops, and how much it influences your ideas and behaviour.

- The Attitude-Life Connection: Learn how closely your attitude and the life you lead are related. Learn how a shift in mindset may transform your experiences.

- The Science of Attitude: Explore the psychology and neurology that underlie attitude, giving the concepts in the book a scientific basis.

- Types of Attitudes: Determine your present attitude by classifying attitudes into three main categories: positive, negative, and neutral.

- The Advantages of Positivity: - Cultivating a Positive Attitude: Learn practical steps to transform your attitude, from changing thought patterns to practising gratitude and managing stress. - Recognize the concrete benefits of a positive attitude, from improved health and relationships to increased resilience and overall happiness.

- Overcoming Difficulties and Obstacles: Overcome difficulties by coping with failures, criticism, and rejection; develop resilience; and convert difficulties into opportunities.

- Establishing and Reaching Goals: As your ally, set specific objectives, maintain motivation, monitor your development, and enjoy your victories with the appropriate mindset.

- Attitude in Professional Life: Examine how attitude affects leadership, networking, and career growth tactics in the workplace.

- Attitude in Personal Life: Utilize attitude concepts in parenting, mental health, personal development, and relationships with others.

- Maintaining Your Upbeat Outlook: Attitude mastery is a continuous process. Create successful routines, place a high value on lifelong learning, surround oneself with encouraging people, and cultivate inner tranquillity.

- Mastering Your Right Attitude: Recognize how your attitude can motivate people, create a lasting impression, and serve as the foundation for the masterpiece that is your life.

3. Approach to Reading: Bear the following points in mind as you set out on this journey:

- Self-Reflection: Take a moment to reflect on yourself after each chapter. Consider incorporating the chapter's lessons into your daily life. With everything you've learnt, how can you change for the better?

- Practical Exercises and Actionable Steps: This book contains exercises and actionable steps. As you read, resolve to give these exercises a try. Transformation requires application.

- Making Notes: Write down your ideas, queries, and epiphanies. Note your observations in the book's margins or a different notebook.

- Talk: Consider discussing the book with friends, family, or classmates. The effect of the content can be increased by exchanging knowledge and experiences.

4. Creating a Positive Habit: Cultivating a positive outlook is crucial, and this is one of the book's main lessons. The secret to long-lasting transformation is consistency. Seize the chance to use the principles of this book consistently and make it a vital part of your road towards happiness and success.

5. Your Trip: "Mastering the Right Attitude: A Guide to Success and Happiness" is a manual that should be followed rather than merely read. This is a personal journey you are on, and the book is a tool to help you realize your potential and goals.

Finally! I can finally take that much-needed beach trip this year, knowing that my extra weight is normal. You did indeed hear me. I'm typical!

How am I aware of this, too? Since this season, several extremely large high-street fashion retailers have begun to highlight fuller-figured women in their swimsuit advertisements. It took a while, but happily, women of all shapes and sizes are now represented in the media as gorgeous, seductive, and, most importantly, acceptable while wearing swimwear.

It appears that you may wear a stylish bikini and yet feel good about your curves without having the physique of a prepubescent 14-year-old.

How long will it take you to accept how your body looks?

You likely have mixed feelings about it, or at least some. Too-large thighs? Too little of a butt? Not enough room in the chest? Is stomach fat uncomfortable? Too thin all around? The majority of women have an obsession with certain parts of their bodies, dissecting them into distinct areas as though they were meat joints. You probably think that while you have some good and some negative characteristics, your life would be so much better if you just had the ideal butt, stomach, or legs.

We'll look at why this myth is so false later. It's an intriguing one that many women of all ages have fallen for. This is a book about women and the challenges they encounter. However, guys can also have negative body image issues and many of the difficulties that affect women, like eating disorders and body shaming.

Many women may also hate their weight in general and be completely committed to altering it. People will stop at nothing to attain their goals of being taller, shorter, firmer, fitter, slimmer, or even younger-looking. Women will go to great measures to battle the fat wars, including bizarre weight-reducing items, taxing miracle workouts, quirky diet fads, and expensive cosmetic surgery. Don't bother focusing on your inner self-worth and confidence because you need a gorgeous body to be happy, right? We live this narrative—with society and ourselves—an ongoing struggle.

It's probably time to fly the white flag and accept who you are.

That does not entail overindulging in food, skipping workouts, or failing to care for oneself. Your mental and physical well-being, confidence, and general well-being depend on all. But you can reach a much better place without all the stress if you can eliminate the need to be something you are not (and maybe never will be).

These are ten fascinating facts regarding body image and how it impacts women, who derive a lot of their cues from the media, friends, family, and social pressure.

In the US, 91% of women claim to be dissatisfied with their bodies and attempt dieting to get the figure they want. Still, just 5 per cent of women naturally have the ideal body type that the media in America portrays.

People who don't eat correctly and are dissatisfied with their bodies may eventually develop eating disorders, which include bingeing, purging, fasting, and continuous dieting.

Over one-third of those who admit to "normal dieting" will later engage in pathological dieting, and 25% of those individuals will eventually experience either a partial or complete eating disorder.

Adolescents who have low self-esteem and contemplate suicide and start dating at a young age.

Those with eating problems typically range in age from 12 to 25 by a staggering 95%.

According to the data above, 58% of college-age girls report feeling pressured to maintain a specific weight.

Young girls' perceptions of their bodies are significantly influenced by reality TV, and the more of it they watch, the more probable it is that they will focus on how they look.

Students who are more exposed to popular media than other female students place more value on beauty and sexiness than on aptitude.

More than 40% of women and almost 20% of men said they would contemplate cosmetic surgery in the future, according to a survey on the topic. Not many variations were seen in age, marital status, or race.

Unfortunately, only approximately 10% of people with eating disorders will seek professional assistance.

UNDERSTAND SELF-ESTEEM

The theme of self-esteem is associated with an individual's high sense of accomplishment or importance. Put another way, self-esteem is the trust and value you place in yourself, independent of external events. Your sense of self-worth influences your actions, relationships, mental health, and overall wellbeing. It affects your motivation as well. People with a healthy, positive self-image are motivated to take on new projects with zest and vigour because they can see their aptitude and talents.

Self-esteem is a contentious subject. Some call it the secret to their success, while others dismiss it as meaningless jargon. You should consider how important self-esteem is to your life and what steps you may take to strengthen it. It's critical to distinguish self-efficacy from self-esteem—your confidence in your capacity to manage predictable situations, actions, or abilities.

If a magic spell could give you a stronger, more positive sense of self-worth, the world would be fairer. But no amount of praise from others can provide you with meaningful, long-term self-esteem; there is no such miracle. Lastly, unless you want them to and want to put in the effort yourself, this book contains no slogans, exercises, or tips that will instantly make you better. There's no shortcut. If you read this guide and don't do the exercises (which are challenging but doable, I assure you), you are losing out.

Self-worth is as vast as the forest, as gloomy as the coral reefs, and fleeting as the waves. Creating goals for yourself, following through on your action plan, and concentrating on the important aspects of your life are all strategies to increase your sense of worth.

How Does One Get Self-Esteem?

Self-esteem has been a major topic of study in contemporary psychology for many years. In therapy, it's a topic that is regularly discussed. Despite much information on the topic, we tend to discuss it in flowery, superficial terms. Genetics, upbringing, life setbacks, peer group dynamics, and, most importantly, our beliefs impact our self-esteem.

Our brains begin to develop the ability to comprehend other people's perceptions (both mentally and visually) from the age of two or three. The medial prefrontal cortex (mPFC) usually begins to mature at this stage of our lives. Theory of mind, individual awareness, and self-identity depend on the mPFC. Therefore, the mPFC is a crucial area for comprehending ourselves and others. At this point, a toddler starts to get interested in spinning in circles but doesn't realize that not every guest who comes over has the same desire to spin. Children begin to pick up on environmental cues around the age of four or five, and they begin to comprehend that two people with different lifestyles have distinct perspectives and methods of reacting to the same things.

One of the most common scenarios that people in therapy consider to address concerns with their self-esteem is hearing their parents criticize others. When a parent figure speaks negatively about other individuals, a child may quickly come to believe that everyone is judgmental. Conversely, parents prioritizing a caring and positive relationship with their kids help them feel better about themselves as they become older adults. People who believe most care about them are less likely to experience worry and mistrust.

Memories connected to unpleasant emotions and circumstances, especially those that make us feel uneasy, laughed at, or abandoned, are stored in our brains. The brain selects the most important memories for preparing for potential future disasters. Even with the smallest occurrences, negative experiences or disappointments are frequently recalled three times more readily than positive ones. A study found that the brain needs five positive experiences to persuade itself that a single unpleasant event was an isolated incident.

Although it may not seem like much, this is the root cause of high and poor self-esteem.

Discovering Your Actual Self

Although discovering who you are may seem like a selfish objective, it is a selfless process that underpins all we accomplish in life. It's a process of removing layers that don't serve us in life or accurately represent who we are. But it also involves a significant act of building, which is deciding who we want to be and pursuing our specific objective with all our might, whatever that may be.

Finding our genuine selves is a question of embracing our inner power while being open to our experiences. There's nothing to fear or steer clear of, and there's no need to be too harsh on yourself while doing it. Rather, use it as an opportunity to learn about yourself like you would if you were meeting someone new.

Have you ever caught a glimpse of yourself through someone else's eyes when you gazed in the mirror? Have you ever thought about your life story as though it were the story of someone else? You aren't likely to do this daily, but have you ever done it? Have you ever entertained the possibility that you are more than one version of yourself?

The term "self" can refer to various roles, including a mother, father, daughter, wife, husband, aunt, uncle, friend, adventurer, seeker, teacher, student, leader, or follower. You might not always be those things as you move between roles and settings. You have a public and a private self, which is even deeper.

This exacerbates the already serious issue of low self-esteem. When you are alone and in public, you perceive and respond to the environment around you differently. Your upbringing, surroundings, and values influence your different selves. Even if you are blind to it, this could have a major negative impact on you. You might lose effort, authenticity, and self-worth if you have two identities.

Look at this straightforward example: Imagine you and your pals are at a party, and they want you to join them on the dance floor and have a little dance. You might object and avoid this suggestion because of your awful dancing abilities or because you don't want your friends to make fun of you if you can't dance. Regardless of your motivations, dancing in public is simply unacceptable. This falls under the category of your public self.

Another situation is when you're alone with your family or a reliable buddy. Any happy or thrilling news may cause you to dance at first. You don't care if you're a terrible dancer at that point since you don't feel the need to hide or worry about your family critiquing your performances. You are expressing your secret self at that precise moment.

While this scenario may not apply to your situation, you can still identify it. Exactly who are you? Who are you When you're alone or in a closed space? It's been said that the true "you" emerges when no one is looking. Which person do you pretend to be—the cheerful, outgoing one you were at school today or the sombre, silent one you were at a party last week? The answer to that question is unique to you. Even if you may not have all the answers now, you can always count on the fact that who you are is distinct, interesting, meaningful, and special.

You can be anxious to show yourself to the world because you think someone will criticize or embarrass you. To avoid being seen or, at the absolute least, to blend in with the crowd, you could pretend to be someone you're not. Individuals with high self-esteem have mastered the art of uniting their private and public selves into a single, intimate link, eliminating any distinction between them. Do you exist as yourself, or are you acting as someone else? Do you behave in a way that makes other people feel good about themselves, or are you more concerned with staying true to who you are?

When you try to be someone or accomplish something for other people, your self-esteem suffers. You know the internal conflict that arises when you defy your instincts. You realize that your "public self" has triumphed over your true self. Your self-esteem rises as you learn to always be your best self and make an effort to be your one genuine self.

www.ingramcontent.com/pod-product-compliance
Lightning Source LLC
Chambersburg PA
CBHW052144110526
44591CB00012B/1849